Being Grateful is the simplest step to reaching a positive state of being. Once you find even the smallest reason to be grateful, more reasons will reveal themselves, you will feel elevated, and those close to you will benefit as well.

Table of Contents

Dedication

To the awakening of our curiosity enough to ask the questions, when we know there is more to the story.

To the awareness that amazing answers will flow in once the void of a question has been created.

Acknowledgments

To my parents, Sam and Barbara Buck, my wife Jane, our children, and grandchildren, I am indeed a lucky man to have you in my life, and you are loved deeply.

I am also grateful for the editing help and encouragement gained from the following people: Bill & Rita Ament, Charlie Buck, Jane Buck, Judith Carter, Sharon Duncan, Sharon Hooper, and Deborah Neff.

About the Author

I was raised on San Juan Island in NW Washington State, access to which is via water and air. I had a wonderful childhood hiking along shorelines and inland adventures knowing I had nothing to fear. No crime, predatory animals or poison plants to worry about. Bees and red ants were about it.

At age 12, we moved to a waterfront farm, where we eventually had horses and cattle. I would steer the tractor to pick up hay bales and as I got older, I fed the animals, helped in much more meaningful ways to bring in the hay, along with keeping the yard mowed.

I did not do well in school and much later in life learned that I was dyslexic which released a lot of guilt and stress stored within in me.

I worked with the County Road crew for two summers running all sorts of equipment including, big trucks, a rock crusher, and a compactor roller for new roads. When we would fly from one island to the next, the piolet would let me fly shortly after leaving the ground.

After two unsuccessful efforts to go to college, I came back to the island and lived in a rough single walled cabin with no utilities and an outhouse for 3 years, working as a bulldozer operator clearing land and digging ponds. Next, I became a commercial fisherman, eventually running a boat by myself. Towards the end of that period I became interested in natural health (Polarity Therapy), which led to me becoming a practitioner. Friends and I bought and operated a restaurant for a couple of years which was a blast. I took a very insightful advanced Polarity course, met my wife and we both worked with that organization for close to 10 years while having our first child in January of 1980.

Upon leaving that organization, I made a valiant effort as a Multilevel Marketer representing Washington State, but the company failed and then we were broke at 38, which was very embarrassing. Fortunately, I became a Realtor about 6 months before the start of a booming market, and that got me back on my feet and has been my career for the last 33 years.

I've been a seeker of truth for most of my life, even as a young teenager. I was raised as a Christian, yet the hell and damnation dogma did not align with my sense of our evolutionary process. I finally found a source affirming my sense of life at 18, through reading Jonathan Livingston Seagull, and I read that book to many of my friends.

This book is really about opening doors and stimulating questions. Each of us must follow life as it pulls us and it is actually impossible to get it wrong, because every event is a teaching moment to do more or do less of what we are experiencing.

The Telephone Experience

Eighty plus percent of the people I have encountered have had the "telephone experience": as you reach for the telephone to call a friend, it rings, and your friend is on the other end of the line, or some variation thereof. You already knew what I was talking about as soon as I mentioned it because it is such a common event. Culturally, we refer to each of these experiences as "an amazing coincidence," but they happen so many times that most of us know down deep there is something happening that goes way beyond "a coincidence." This does not mean that most of us are ready to climb aboard the good ship—*paranormal;* it just means that we are on the verge of publicly accepting that there is much more to our lives than we or mainstream science have been willing to acknowledge.

What is the medium through which these telepathic-like events happen? What are the implications of fully accepting and embracing that, at least to some degree, we are all telepathic?

What cultural dynamics are in place that keep the vast majority of the scientific community resistant to acknowledging that telepathy exists?

By far, most scientists say that such a thing is nonsense, and they will go on to cast aspersions towards the few scientists who seriously investigate these events.

When I talked to a scientist about this subject, he said that *if any form of telepathy was proven to be real, it would completely change our fundamental understanding of how the universe works*. He made that statement as if it would almost be a sin to do so and implied that I was naïve for even bringing such an idea up in his presence.

As you will read a little further along, the evidence is so overwhelming; it actually seems bizarre that mainstream science keeps trying to pretend that these telepathic-like events do not exist when for most of us, such an event is so commonplace, we cannot deny the evidence.

Aside from the telephone experience, are there any other aspects of this amazing medium of communication that we are experiencing? Of course! What about the common acceptance of a mother's ability to sense her child's well-being? The mothers who have had an out-of-the-blue, very strong sense that something has happened are very clear about it, and have many times been correct. When a mother's feelings are validated, she has an experience that is not explainable by 90 to 95% of today's scientists.

What is it about who we are that keeps us from accepting that our direct experiences are as real as the earth we are standing on? Who is a better judge of what is real than us?

Having trusted people to ask questions of is wonderfully important and should be encouraged. In doing so, one must also remember that such people are speaking only from their experience or maybe even just theoretical experience, so all they can do is reflect possibilities that may or may not align with one's own sense of what's true.

When the answers of trusted teachers are not a match to our sense of what is true, our sense of security is challenged, and we become vulnerable to losing trust in ourselves. That specific moment is one of the most important moments of life to teach our children about. It is not a question of the intent or integrity of the advisor with whom one may have been very aligned. It is a question of allowing for and trusting our own personal evolution.

We know when the answers are the right ones; we feel the harmonic alignment. When the frequency of the answer given aligns with our frequency, it's like striking a tuning fork that matches our note. Such experiences are wonderful moments as we know we are experiencing truth for us in that moment of time. These are the self-guiding aspects of life that are so important for our children to learn. Let us help them to pay attention to, and follow, that which they are in harmony with.

What aspect of ourselves allows us to feel such harmonics? How far does our ability extend, and what is it that we are feeling? Do our sensitivities extend to feeling the frequencies of other life forms? What is the definition of other life forms? Is such a connection a two-way street?

Think about the impact of constantly validating each other. What if we openly taught our children to pay attention to these other means of communication? What if we had been doing so for generations? When would be a good time to start?

Once fully engaged, I am sure that this field of science will lead to some of the biggest and most life-changing breakthroughs of all time. The few scientists that have taken on the challenge are among the most highly credentialed pioneering scientists alive, and they are coming up with possibilities that may turn into answers.

God? Inter-Active Intelligence?

Even though there are many perceptions of what God is, all seem to agree that God is "all-knowing." Some say they do not believe in a God, at least as represented to them. From observation, I sense that even most believers are not exactly that clear about how it all works, so they rely on faith to sustain them. Is there a bridge between the two positions?

As a means of finding some common ground for the purpose of communication in this book, I propose the following possibility as a baseline:

I believe in the existence of collective inter-active intelligence that is sourced through the frequencies emanated by all that exists. The degree to which we are personally and collectively aware of these interactions is the measure of our personal and collective consciousness.

How far does that collective intelligence extend? What is the definition of "all that exists"? How much do we even understand about the very nature or source of that collective consciousness?

For many, the need to understand their individual and collective strong feelings of being a part of something larger than themselves has been, and continues to be, a driving force leading to many theories and certainties about who God is and how it all works.

I believe in the truth each of us seeks to understand and in the evolution of that awareness.

I also believe that there is overwhelming evidence that we are clearly interacting with each other through a physical medium of exchange that we scarcely understand.

As in every aspect of our lives, there will always be people who know more about a given subject than we do. Those beings with the most knowledge radiate a frequency signature that communicates their level of understanding.

When one is just beginning to learn the basics of a given subject, it is highly unlikely that one would be able to interpret the frequency generated from a being that is radiating a much more advanced level of understanding, although the more advanced being would have the ability to relate to the beginner's level.

How many fields of learning are you aware of?

How many levels of development are there within that field? How many fields of learning exist that we have yet to become cognizant of?

Whenever I refer to God in this offering, please consider God to be the source of the frequency signature that emanates the fullest state of comprehension of love and all that exists.

When I refer to the soul, I am referring to that part of our perceived individuality that is intimately connected to the collective intelligence/God frequency at the most "knowing" level.

I like the electricity analogy. The same energy medium that provides for the simplest of uses also animates the most complex devices, and in all cases, it is stepped down from a greater source.

To me, God is the sum total of all that exists, and the richness of our experience is limited only by our beliefs.

Happenings

By some blend of mind and soul, we are given hints or inspirations to encourage us towards a better way forward.

Through modest inquiry, I've discovered that more people than you might have guessed have had, what are for them, undeniable, direct experiences with elevated beings. These beings expressed themselves through a variety of forms and provided those fortunate people with valuable insights and/or timely communications.

The people I am referring to are very successful people of all faiths who appear to be, in every other aspect, as normal as apple pie, and most of the time, such people will share their experience only when they feel it is "safe" to do so. Since many of us are void of a like-kind experience, we tend to categorize such an event as "a psychosis," as we have no other point of reference.

For the benefit of both, a possible distinguishing factor between one and the other might be the uplifting personal insights and the distinct perception of "truth" or "knowing" that accompanies such an experience.

These happenings are disruptive to our foundational teachings, and therefore, over time, our subconscious mind will do its best to either bury or disguise the event. I know this from personal experience.

Even though historically, our cultures have come up with many ways and names to describe such profound events, does calling them one thing or another change what happened?

Were those brief moments meant to provide insights as to what is possible by simply learning to attune our frequencies?

I accept any experience in this physical world as an indication of what is possible to repeat by understanding the means through which it became manifest.

What are the reaches of the medium that allows telepathic communications? Do we need to seriously expand our concept of what "physical" means? Are some of what we might consider being "spiritual experiences" simply elevated physical experiences? Where is the line between the two? Does there need to be a line?

Bravery & The Odds

It takes great bravery to break step with convention, as by doing so, one submits oneself to the risk of criticism, ridicule, and alienation to the point of being treated as an outcast. Since history bears this out so well, I encourage both those outcasts on the cutting edge and those equally hard-working souls inside the more comfortable circle of the convention to be more appreciative of each other's state of being. We are who we are, and the process is the process, so compassion is deserved in a full circle.

The frontier can be lonely and yet very rewarding. We all play our different parts, often for reasons yet to be revealed. We are all on the frontier of our own life experience.

It will not be long until the few courageous scientists who are doing this work will be followed by droves of their peers, rushing to explain how that which most of us are experiencing can actually happen.

As implied earlier, current scientific protocols do not allow for the possibility of telepathy, so to acknowledge that any kind of "telepathic" event even exists is incredibly disruptive to the current foundation on which science stands.

It is difficult to build on anything less than a solid foundation. The current foundation has already been torn down and reconstructed many times, so as a means of maintaining the status quo, most scientists say that what is perceived as a "telepathic telephone experience" is nothing more than statistical odds.

Think about it: what are the odds that within a few seconds of an entire week or month, Sue just happens to pick up the telephone to call Sally at the very moment Sally was calling Sue?

If, like so many others, you have had Telepathic Telephone Experiences (TTEs) over and over again, you have no doubt that your experience was much more than an odds event. Such odds are more along the lines of winning the lottery, and that certainly does not happen to the majority of us over and over again.

Paradigm Shift

Even though TTEs are familiar events, for most of us, it is still a little "out there" to fully admit to ourselves, or anyone else, that we have always possessed another extraordinary yet very fundamental system of communication.

As our collective minds are opening, we realize that we absolutely know that this other form of communication does exist. As each individual integrates this information, yet another piece of the puzzle falls into place. Those extra data points provide missing links in our logical processing center, which allows us to be more confident in our conclusions about this life we are living.

Just like any new shift in our reality, it takes a little while to become comfortable. I liken it to walking out of a dark room into the light of a bright day; once our eyes adjust to the brighter light, we are free to feast on the richness of what lies before us. I believe that analogy is indicative of just how much our lives are about to change.

We are at the beginning of another renaissance, and within a few more years, we may look back on this time as the ending of a period of relative darkness.

The TTE event is simple, fun, and commonly experienced, yet the broad implications are so far-reaching it takes most people a little time to fully comprehend and engage what will be, for most of the scientific community, literally a whole new avenue of legitimate science.

How rare it is to have the opportunity to witness the beginning of a whole new field of science, particularly one that has such direct influence on our daily lives.

As a result of one little adjustment in our neural synaptic wiring, we find ourselves on the precipice of a huge and magnificent canyon, taking in a view that is vast and inspiring, if not a bit startling.

As you can tell, I believe this simple cultural experience has yet to be recognized for the deep and very powerful part it is contributing towards the flashpoint of the paradigm shift we are on the verge of experiencing.

It is not just that TTEs happen; it is how often they happen. As a culture, we have become so saturated with this experience that we simply have no choice but to acknowledge the truth of it.

Admitting such knowledge, in a world where our credibility can be at stake for just talking about such things, reveals a little insight as to what those cutting-edge scientists have been up against.

When we get past the cutesy part of it all, the truth of this subject becomes a catalyst for the major expansion of our personal understanding of the universe we live in.

What other thoughts are we broadcasting and receiving? By improving our thoughts, do we have a positive influence on others? If we can pick up on another's intent to call us, what else are we picking up on?

Ten or twenty years from now, I think we will look back at this moment in time as being within the flashpoint of a very exciting and significant change.

A flashpoint happens after a significant percentage (33%? 51%?) of a population accepts a new way of thinking, and then, almost seamlessly, the balance of the population appears to accept the change as if the "new way" is the way it has always been.

We are turning a corner and moving towards an enhanced understanding of our individual and collective power. We are learning that we have the possibility to influence the health, peace, and well-being of ourselves and our planet.

The common telephone will turn out to have been the avenue that allowed us to move past reinforced thought barriers with very little resistance.

So many of the barriers we accept as real are nothing more than a movie being projected onto a thin veil that our perceptions interpret as our reality.

Only when some outside force creates a ripple in the veil does the illusion start to become apparent, and that is when the door to our mind opens through our curiosity. Soon we find ourselves looking behind the screen to behold new territories for discovery where more questions and answers to the mysteries of our lives will be revealed.

What Is The Medium?

What is the medium that allows N'kisi the parrot to call out the names of pictures being observed by people that the parrot has no way of seeing?

I discussed this event with the same accomplished scientist mentioned earlier. He replied that what I had witnessed was "nothing more than smoke and mirrors, just a magician's trick". He also remarked, "If such an event were real, it would completely disrupt the foundation of current science." People only react like that when their foundational beliefs are being threatened, which means to me that even though he sensed the truth, he did not want me to disrupt his beliefs, which we are all guilty of.

What is the medium that allows so many dogs and other animals to change from whatever they are doing in favor of moving to a door or window 20 minutes prior to their owners' arrival, when all other possible explanations have been eliminated?

What is the medium and accompanying process of communication that enables most of us to experience such a direct connection with another human being? What communication process is taking place when we pick up the telephone to call someone, the very same person is actually already on the line surprised that the telephone was picked up before they even heard a single ring?

How do most of us respond to these phenomena? We say, "I can't believe it, I was just dialing you." What keeps us from believing what we experience?

For most of us, just talking about these kinds of events puts us out of our comfort zone and creates social risk. To compensate, we have learned to disassociate by saying, "What a coincidence!" or "Isn't that amazing?"

Social risk tends to keep us marching in "lock step". In general bringing up alternative ideas can become controversial very quickly, either through cultural perceptions of science or religion, and since usually the challenger is more versed and convinced about that their perception is correct, we know the faster the subject gets dropped, the better. Social resistance holds back support for scientific research; hence, my purpose for publishing this book.

Change is happening, as evidenced by the fact that more and more of us are starting to make increasingly accurate comments in response to some obvious connectivity, such as, "Wow, we are really tuned in to each other" or "We must really be on the same wavelength."

Everything that we know emits a unique and measurable frequency signature. Can we change what we emit? Can we hone our abilities to receive and interpret the myriad of frequencies that are being emitted by objects in our environment? What are our chances of improving those abilities when we have yet to commonly accept that such possibilities exist? Think of how exciting it would be once we finally discover how to describe and quantify this medium. Is there a limit to our abilities? As in any field of endeavor, are there those who truly excel through practice? Yes.

Other Events

Currently, there are many experiential and scientifically undeniable examples that demonstrate other dimensions of the "telepathic telephone experience".

Dr. Rupert Sheldrake has been documenting some of these phenomena for many years and has written numerous books on the subject, including *Dogs That Know When Their Owners Are Coming Home* and *The Sense of Being Stared At.* You might crack a smile about those titles. However, these events have been documented using scientific protocols and are fun to read about, in addition to being quite revealing.

Dr. Sheldrake points out that since we spend so much time with our pets, it is not unreasonable that we would discover more about the nature of our relationship with animals through our experiences with our pets.

Many cases have been documented of dogs and other animals demonstrating through their behavior that they know when their owners are coming home significantly ahead of their arrival. After eliminating all other possible explanations, these experiments were able to demonstrate that a dog will go and stand at the door, as it always does, 20 minutes prior to its owner's arrival.

Dr. Sheldrake provided evidence of such an event with the help of two synchronized video machines that simultaneously recorded the actions of the owner and her pet dog. The owner of the dog was taken to a town approximately a 20-minute drive away. Dr. Sheldrake asked his assistants to go for a walk around the town with the owner, and then, at a random time, affirmed with her that it was now time to return to her home. As the woman verbally confirmed with the assistants that they were going to go home, the split-screen revealed that the dog got up, stretched, and then stood by the door until she arrived back home, just as it had always done 20 minutes before her return.

This demonstration and six others are available for viewing via Dr. Sheldrake's video tape, *Seven Experiments That Can Change the World.*

In the same manner, Dr. Sheldrake has documented the talents of an African grey parrot named N'kisi. The bird has a vocabulary of more than 1,200 words and has demonstrated that it can describe, in precise English, photographs that its owner is looking at for the first time in a separate room at the opposite end of the house, out of sight of the parrot.

As of this writing, that parrot is five years old and many well-known and trusted people, including Jane Goodall, have witnessed this phenomenon. Undoubtedly, you will be hearing more about this bird, as it has to be one of the most dramatic demonstrations of a phenomenon that we all need to understand more about.

What About Miracles?

I believe in miracles in a different way than most people do. I see them as hints from God that are meant to demonstrate what is possible through our natural abilities. Rather than be amazed and dig into how what happened really happened, we call it a miracle, kind of like using the word "coincidence" and it gets a little more attention. "These things just happen." Most MD's explanation.

Several cases of miraculous recoveries from any number of terrible conditions have been documented over the years. The most profound of these are called "spontaneous remissions", which can literally be described as overnight recoveries, and as such, have completely confounded the medical community.

If we were really paying attention when just one of those events occurred, it would have become front-page news. Furthermore, with full recognition of the implied humanitarian benefits, we might have launched a national effort, along the lines of NASA's moon expedition, to discover how it happened and how we could repeat it at will.

Instead of taking such actions, we tend to place these events on the religious shelf with so many other misunderstood subjects. Once a phenomenon is placed there, who will risk being called a heretic for trying to dissect God? Who will jeopardize their professional standing by openly giving the event serious consideration?

There is a story that indirectly illustrates one possible answer:

A man was flailing in the water, trying to keep from drowning, when a boat came along and offered to pull him aboard. He answered, "God will save me", so the boat moved along. Soon another boat came along and offered to pull his exhausted body on board, and he answered, “God will save me, God will save me.” So that boat also moved along. Eventually, the man drowned. When he met God, he asked, “Why didn’t you save me?” God looked at him lovingly and said, “I sent two boats.”

Trying to understand the mechanism by which a body can heal spontaneously is not akin to an attempt at dissecting God. On the contrary, such an effort would be an appropriate response to one of the many directional signs God places in our path towards enlightenment.

We live in a physical world. When something happens in our physical world, it often has a physical answer, even if we are yet to understand the full extent of what “physical” means.

I believe that many of what are perceived as “miraculous events” are actually pretty obvious hints as to what is possible to achieve. So far, we just seem to be a little slow on the uptake.

What keeps our culture from being totally excited about the undeniable evidence of how much more there is to understand? What prevents us from dedicating as much time, energy, and research to this subject as it deserves? Think of how much suffering we could eliminate if we became seriously committed, with less fear and more vigor, to understanding the process by which "medical miracles" happen.

As far as I can determine, the "placebo effect" might be another example of what we refer to as "a miracle". Science tends to refer to them as annoyances because they get in the way of collecting "true data".

According to research reported by Dr. Bruce Lipton, lecturer and author of *The Biology of Belief*, records (gained through the Freedom of Information Act) reveal that some of the most heavily advertised pharmaceutical drugs have produced only modestly better results than the placebo. Add to that slight edge a huge advertising campaign to convince people that the drugs will work, and the placebo aspect of the drug's effectiveness will certainly be enhanced.

It was not long ago that family physicians routinely carried a selection of pills of various sizes and colors to provide relief to their patients via the placebo effect. Were those people just pretending to be sick, or were they truly sick and recovered because of their belief in the power of the good doctor's prescription?

I witnessed video tapes of two men who had experienced the same invasive dental procedure, with the exception that Bob had been given a pain pill that was a placebo whereas Bill was told that certain circumstances prevented him from being able to take a pain pill. Bob sat around casually reading a magazine, but Bill clearly showed signs of suffering, such as moaning and holding his hand to his jaw.

The placebo effect is simply another example of one of those hints. With nothing more than the power of suggestion and a sugar pill, our minds create an effect to match the power of a strong medication. What else might our minds be able to accomplish? How many untapped abilities do we have?

If we learn how to create the desired effect without putting toxic substances into our bodies, how different could our hospitals become? What other skill sets might our doctors receive training in?

As noted previously, until recently, our culture, including our scientists, have treated these events as novelties. We say, “Well, these things just happen sometimes” and, with few exceptions, that is as far as we have gone.

I am very enthusiastic about where we stand presently in our development. I believe that we are on the verge of grasping a new understanding of the very nature of our being and the universe we live in.

When reading about the past, our grandchildren might compare the significance of the paradigm shift we are going through now to what it was like for our ancestors to realize, for instance, that instead of the sun moving around the Earth, the Earth moves around the sun. Think of how monumental it would have been for that culture to reorient their perception of the way the world works, and the far-reaching implications of that discovery was for civilization. When that paradigm shifted, think of how many barriers to thought were dropped and how much further our ancestors' thinking could expand.

Electromagnetic Fields?

The book *The Heart's Code* by Paul Pearsall refers to a study of 2,000 people who received heart transplants. The study found that two-thirds of those people took on some of the distinctive characteristics of the donors despite having no previous knowledge about them. What is the actual medium that would allow such a thing to happen? In one case a woman had received the heart of someone who had been murdered. Shortly thereafter, she started to have memories of the murder in enough detail that the information she shared ultimately led to the capture of the murderer.

Is there something like an electromagnetic field around our living tissue that encompasses our memories and behavior patterns? How big could these fields be? How far might they extend from our bodies? When two fields are close enough, could there be an exchange of intelligence? Could "close enough" have two meanings, both physical and emotional?

What if a heart transplant is also somewhat of a brain transplant, as has recently been proposed by Dr. Pearsall? Did you know that the heart is formed prior to the brain? What if a preceding energy pattern is what actually creates the heart and the brain? What is the source of that intelligence? Where is the beginning? Where is the end? How is that energy pattern created and how much is stored there?

Even though most of us still believe that our chromosomes function like the brain of our cells, cutting-edge science implies that they work more along the lines of a chemical plant that responds to another set of impulses coming from across the membrane, or mem-"brain", as Dr. Bruce Lipton further describes in his book *The Biology of Belief*. He states that science has believed that the cell membrane functions only as a semi-permeable protective skin that holds the fluids in and keeps sodium levels balanced. Dr. Lipton proved that the cell membrane is a highly complex structure and is charged with a vast array of duties that more closely resemble the attributes we had thus far assigned to the chromosomes.

Where is intelligence stored and how is it accessed? Are we simply a mass of innumerable intelligent frequencies manifesting out of vortexes of energy or photons of light? Dr. Bruce Lipton refers to this idea and, from what I can gather, there is little chance that we are anything else.

As I read in *The Power of Prayer* by Larry Dossey, a double-blind study was carried out which documented the effectiveness of prayer on men who had experienced heart attacks. The results were so positive that, had the study been based on a pill of some sort, it would have been considered a major breakthrough.

The most effective prayer was, “Thy will be done,” and neither religious affiliation nor being religious were determined to be distinguishing factors. The most important characteristic associated with the effectiveness of the practitioner was the degree to which one exhibited a positive attitude.

It did not matter if practitioners were standing right next to the patient, outside the room, or in another state; the effectiveness was the same.

Vibrational Beings

Even though it may seem intangible, there is power in our intention. The evidence keeps mounting that our thoughts are not mere things rolling around inside our heads. We all emit a distinct, measurable frequency, as does each cell of our body. As frequencies are vibrational patterns, I submit that we are all indeed vibrational beings that emit and receive frequencies.

Everything in our universe has a frequency signature, even thoughts or ideas. The more we focus on what we like or what we don't, the more support we are providing to those energizing impulses that effectively increase the mass and power of the same.

If you want something to become more powerful, feed it energy. If you would like it to become less powerful, stop paying any attention to it.

Whether your attention is stimulated from a positive place or a negative one, attention equals energy, and therefore, expansion.

If we consider all aspects of life as thought forms, then, for the sake of illustration, let's pretend our thought forms to be like the plants in our garden, and the attention we give to them as light and water. If we focus our attention on the weeds in our lives, we energize them and help them expand. With discipline, however, we can choose to focus that life-sustaining attention on the parts of life that provide us with enriched sustenance.

This analogy applies to us individually, culturally, nationally, and globally. It is not about pretending that the weeds are not there; it is about using our consciousness to focus on what we want to grow and expand. As we become more conscious, we grasp how important "positive thought" is to the quality of our individual and collective lives. With proper training and focus, the produce in our gardens becomes so large and full of vitality that the weeds of our lives tend to become less obvious or simply wither away for lack of attention.

Our Programming

According to research, our subconscious mind governs most of each day's activities based on the programming we've previously accepted. As a means of being able to learn the language and social mores of the subculture we are born into, from the time we are conceived up until when we are seven years old, we operate like a holographic recording machine that imprints everything we are exposed to as "the way the world is," without question or discrimination, just as a dry sponge will draw in any liquid without regard to its purity.

Our parents, their parents, and so on, were all imprinted upon before they had a chance to discriminate between positive, negative, good, bad, etc. This makes it easy to understand how positive and negative patterns are passed along within a family.

Those underlying patterns of behavior are then modified by our reactions to life and by life's reactions to us. They form our current habit patterns. Most of our actions stem from our subconscious foundational understanding of life, which essentially comes from our early programming.

This imprinting is so strong that it is not uncommon to hear, "That is just the way I am," which is true until we understand our options.

The degree to which we understand and accept our current programming is the degree to which we have the freedom to change.

As our conscious mind seeks that freedom, we can find excellent methods of decoupling ourselves from the old programs. We can replace programs that no longer serve us with new ones that give us the tools we need to accomplish what we truly desire. We have a choice in every moment.

There is substantial evidence to prove that we are fairly programmable, and I would venture to say that advertising companies made that same conclusion long ago. Since we have accepted our current programming without the benefit of critical decision-making, maybe it is time to consider the options.

To review, the understanding that the way we live our life is mostly based on deep programming is of the utmost importance. We underwent this programming before we could develop any ability to judge positive from negative, right from wrong, fair from unfair, etc. We express our foundational programming through a filter comprising layers of beliefs that we have accepted over the years.

Consciousness is an aspect of life that represents a kind of awakening, whereby we start to have a more objective view of how we came to be who we are. One can make conscious change only to the degree of one's awake-ness.

Upon realizing that we have choices, there are many wonderful and proven means of inserting new programs into the deeper levels of our psyche. Everyone around us is an example of what is possible. Take the time to observe what is attractive to you and then seek the programming that can take you in that direction.

There is growing evidence indicating that simple modifications can create profound changes in the quality of our individual lives. As we change ourselves, we also contribute to the improvement of our collective lives.

Put a new program in and experience it. If you like it, keep it; otherwise, find another one that you like better. We do that with music, movies, and clothes, so it stands to reason that we can do the same with our personal programming as well.

Allow yourself to try on a new perspective to see how it fits. One might fear that by doing so one could irreversibly lose oneself. However, when one tries on a new piece of clothing, one does not "lose oneself"; one just puts it back on the shelf and looks for something more aligned with one's true nature.

You are free to have a relationship with you. This is your life right now. As they say, "This is not a dress rehearsal." The sum experience of your life has brought you to this very moment.

In published accounts of near-death experiences, when people find themselves in the presence of divinity or elevated beings called by many names, they report feeling tremendous love, understanding, and compassion.

While in that state, they report that everything about who they are and every relationship they have ever experienced makes perfect sense to them. Even under those most profound circumstances, they seem to retain a sense of self-identity while discovering more about their true nature.

Take the time to listen to or read about the people who have had such experiences. You will be able to sense if the person is making it all up or whether they are sharing a real and profound experience. I have heard of two such accounts from friends of my mother-in-law who lived in the same retirement center. There are many other written accounts as well. Two that I particularly enjoyed reading are *Embraced by the Light* by Bettie Eddie and *Saved by the Light* by Danion Brinkley.

The evidence suggests to me that the present-time observer aspect of who we are is a constant witness to our lives in a much more expanded capacity than we typically imagine.

This Is Your Journey

This journey you are on is all about you. Every experience is a growth experience for your benefit as well as for the benefit of everyone around you. Every experience leads to a deeper understanding of your true nature and moves you closer to living in joy, peace, and love. Eventually, each of us will come to trust the beautiful, intelligent connectivity of all that is.

Without choices, we feel disempowered and a bit hopeless. Despite how you found yourself reading this little book, your life brought you to this moment.

Hopefully, you are gaining the understanding that you have endless choices and that you have the right and the ability to reprogram yourself to experience that which you would most enjoy.

To put it another way. For most of our waking day, we function through our pre-programmed subconscious mind. The balance of the day is filled with conscious action. I think the following analogy will be helpful in grasping this concept.

Please think of your mind and body as a huge ocean liner cruising to a specific preprogrammed destination.

Think about all of the activities it takes to keep such a ship happy: plumbing, electrical, housekeeping, cooking, operational coordination, and attending to guests who are enjoying the benefits of all the support.

Think about the mass and momentum involved as you are making your way through the sea of life.

The fact is that most of the time, while the captain is sleeping, entertaining, or managing, it is the first mate (our subconscious) who is on the watch to make sure that the ship is staying on the "programmed" course.

When the captain (conscious action) steps back into the wheelhouse to review the charts and progress towards the destination, he can, with a slight adjustment of the wheel, put the ship back on course or adjust the course towards a new destination.

When inspiration is followed by conscious action, our personal as well as our global world benefits from it.

We all have the option, at any time in our lives, to come back into the wheelhouse and change course, regardless of how much momentum there may be in a given direction. All it takes is the realization that there is a more desirable destination, the awareness that along with being a passenger we are also the captain, and the courage to step up to the wheel.

Inspirations

Where does inspiration come from?

There are many levels of inspiration. Some are more subtle, such as receiving a new idea, having a revealing insight, or perceiving the possibility of a new path forward.

Some inspirations are more direct and can even be accompanied by an impulse strong enough to create actual physical movement, such as speaking up to share one's perception, reaching out to touch someone, or writing down something one is becoming cognizant about.

I perceive all inspirations as communications from a higher state of consciousness and as gifts to be appreciated. When we acknowledge those gifts for what they are and follow through with action, we demonstrate that we are fertile soil for those seeds, and that we have the will to energize them. Such action reinforces and strengthens that connection, which in turn increases the flow of similar inspirations.

It is a different take on the finger-in-the-dam story. If you allow the flow to happen, it will continue to grow and become stronger.

The Play

Sometimes I have this sense of being called upon or cued to play a part in a play that I've never read and whose script is revealed to me only a few moments before I am cued for my lines. In those inspired moments and in the midst of my scene, I experience being a part of, and guided by, a collective intelligence. When that happens, and even when it does not, I tend to trust that I have been perfectly cast into the complexity of this comedic action/drama experience called my life, and I think that must be the case for us all.

I have discovered that when I am feeling frustrated, it is only because I am expecting others to execute their parts according to how I would write their script. Every time I find myself in that state, I know that the path to regaining my balance lies in becoming a fascinated observer, excited to see how the play is going to unfold and trusting that others are also being cued to just as I have was in this grand play.

It is like a multidimensional, holographic chess game, except that the outcome is orchestrated in such a manner that everyone gets to play the part they came here to play. So, everyone wins.

I believe that inspirations are sourced from many levels. Where did you get the thought to pick up the phone to call up the person who called you? Could that be categorized as an inspiration? What about feeling compelled to share an important insight that could make a difference in someone's life? Is that all coming from within you or was the other person drawing or conceiving that inspiration through you?

What about the calling to give thanks to a higher source? Almost all cultures through time have felt compelled to do so.

What is the medium through which all of these events occur? Are they linked together by a means we can at least partially understand? I think so.

Are inspirations gifts? Or are they impulses generated by some sort of collective feedback wherein the gift is our ability to receive such feedback? Either way, active appreciation encourages more of the same.

Gravity is a force or medium that literally holds our lives together. You might be surprised to know that science still has six distinct theories about how it really functions, which means they are still working on it.

Gravity is a medium that science has fully acknowledged and studied for a very long time. With that in mind, and since most of us have not even formally acknowledged the existence of this other medium by which we are all connected, it is not surprising that we 1) don't understand more about it, and 2) don't even have a generally accepted name to describe something that is such an intimate part of our lives.

Universal Frequency Field

From the research and studies I've read, and observations I've made to date, I believe that we are living in and are enveloped by a universal frequency field. Within that field, we are all connected by the degree of our attention to, or awareness of, all that exists, be it other people, things, emotions, ideas, or perceptions of reality. Whatever captures our attention will be affected by our attention to it, to a lesser or greater degree, depending upon the emotional force or intent behind it.

If you look at someone for a moment and then look away, that person may not have received enough attention to give you a response. However, if you have ever focused on someone for one reason or another, you know that it does not take long for that person to turn and look directly into your eyes. Most of us have had that happen to us at least a few times in our lives and, in fact, such a response is so predominant that professional investigators are trained to keep looking away to avoid being detected.

Even if you focus on a person and they don't turn around, they might feel that stare, just like you may have, and be resisting the urge to look back, which is still a response that demonstrates a two-way medium of communication whether we name it or not. Ninety percent of you know exactly what I am talking about because it is so experientially predominant.

What other examples of this two-way communication are there?

What about the phenomenon of experiencing everything falling into place, for example, people or events just showing up at the right moment? I believe such experiences happen out of some sort of collaboration within a collective, emerging, dynamic intelligence that keeps connecting the dots of our lives according to the course we have consciously or unconsciously charted. The synchronicity of such undeniable experiences is yet another complex expression of the connectivity demonstrated by the "telepathic telephone experience".

Are we like instruments expressing ourselves through various frequencies in solo or as a symphony?

Let's remember that a symphony is an intelligent organization of many solos. All the players do their best to play their individual parts while experiencing the beauty expressed through their interdependent relationships.

Physicists say that if we looked at an electron, proton, or neutron, we would not see any kind of physical matter. They explain that when we break our universe down into the smallest entities currently possible, literally everything we know of and experience is, in their most basic form, little bits of energy.

In *The Biology of Belief*, Dr. Bruce Lipton states that if we could see an electron or proton, we would see little spinning vortexes of energy. To account for solid materials such as a table or a rock, he points out that if we were speeding down a highway and ran into an invisible tornado at high speed, we would experience hitting something solid.

Everything that exists, including little bits of energy, emits and receives frequency signatures.

How does an antenna and a receiver work? Certain bands of energy waves are sent out at different rates of oscillation. The rates of oscillation describe the height of the peaks and valleys of the waves and their distance from each other. An antenna is created to match those specific waves while ignoring other waves that are passing by. A receiver translates the bits of information coming through that particular frequency into voice, pictures, or any other form of data.

Think about how many man-made energy waves—television, radio, and cellular—are being broadcast through the air right now via land-based and satellite-based broadcast systems all over the world. If you possessed some sort of internal receiver (one is probably being invented right now), you could tune in to and experience any one of those frequencies.

Essentially, everything is made of pure waves of energy that have found dynamic co-operative relationships. Each relationship radiates a frequency signature to identify its availability for further, more complex relationships, and each relationship also has a receiver to find the right harmonizing frequency signatures to cooperate with.

The capacities to broadcast, receive, and translate, at infinite levels of ability and need, represent the essence and very nature of our universe.

Even a rock is the result of a cooperative relationship of masses of electrons and protons spinning around a nucleus (which are all vortexes of energy). If movement or activity is synonymous with being alive, then at some level that rock is “alive”.

A growing number of us are beginning to realize that we were born with a significantly more advanced set of communication skills than we have ever been taught about. Since our parents and teachers had not been taught about this by their parents and teachers, they could not pass it down to us.

As we learn to trust in this subtler aspect of ourselves, we will naturally become more fluent and better able to navigate through our world. In general, I think we can all agree that it is much more fun to travel when you know the language of the land.

As very young children, our capacity to utilize the full scope of our natural abilities is suppressed by the blanket of "historic reality". Most of the time, when we do not understand something, we fear it. We develop stories about the importance of disassociating from that which is not accepted. These stories eventually became cultural fear programs, and we are taught that anything outside of "normal" is abnormal, and anything abnormal can't be good.

Again, since most of our parents and grandparents did not know much about these natural abilities, they certainly could not teach or encourage us to use them. In fact, in most cases, it was seriously considered a taboo subject even if they did have certain knowledge to pass along.

It is socially easier to roll along with a taboo than to question it, or to discover and explain something one has not been educated about. When our children ask us questions, we always want to give them an answer, even when we are not sure of it ourselves. Thus, we tend to give them the answers that we were given, just as our parents did.

"Fifty percent of facts are made up on the spot." I got a real chuckle out of that one the first time I heard this statement, and I believe there is a lot of truth in it.

Through trial and error (conscious or unconscious), we are slowly gaining an understanding of our capabilities. We are learning that we have a marvelous ability to radiate frequencies that communicate who we are as well as our intent. Simultaneously, we are also receiving and interpreting the frequencies emanating from all that surrounds us. Some people are better prepared than others to emanate, receive, and interpret this subtler kind of information. Therefore, they have developed amazing skills that the rest of us have not even conceived of as a possibility.

Physical distance does not seem to be a factor in our ability to communicate via this yet unknown medium. Rather, a TTE seems to be primarily dependent on how emotionally close or mentally aligned we are with someone.

When we think of someone, we visualize some aspect of them, and that event transmits a specific frequency signature relative to that person. That same frequency pattern will quickly find its match via the appropriate receiver, like a key to a lock. Thus, a line of communication is cstablished, whether consciously or unconsciously.

When such a match happens, the recipient might feel a very subtle impulse that leads to a fleeting thought about the sender. If the receiver dwells on the sender for a moment, they return that signal via the matched frequency pattern link-up. If that impulse bounces back and forth a couple of times, it might build enough strength that one or the other may decide to make a call. That intention generates a defined "make-a-telephone-call" frequency pattern, which in turn beams back along that same channel to the other party. When they pick up on that thought pattern, they may experience that message as their own impulse to make the call.

Of course, as one makes the call, the other is reaching out to do the same thing. The phone rings, we answer, and everyone says, "Wow, I was just reaching for the telephone to call you," or something along those lines.

When we think about someone, we tune in to their frequency, which is almost like knocking on their door lightly. The more we focus on them, the more power is generated behind that signal, which correlates to a louder knock on their door.

As in any house, that person may have so much noise within their head, kind of like listening to a radio or television, that they just can't hear the knocking. Others, however, may respond right away.

Thought Forms Are Things

Anything that exists in our universe receives and broadcasts the essence of its existence. I believe that any specific idea, attitude, belief system, or concept is a "thought form" that, once created, exists and maintains a space in our universe.

We all have antennas of some sort that allow us to receive and interpret frequency input, and we all have broadcast equipment that broadcasts who we are in every given second of our existence.

How do we know if we are generating a new thought or picking up on the broadcast signal of an existing and building thought form? To me, that is not an important question. I experience everything that is happening as a collective event. Each one of us is a voice in a choir who may occasionally have what appears to be a solo part. Who wrote the music? Who plays the music? Who are you singing for? How did you learn to sing? What made you even feel like singing?

We all have the ability to pick up frequencies from thought forms of anything that exists in our universe and we are constantly doing so. Since most of us have no other frame of reference, it is common for us to believe that all of our internal thoughts, experiences, and images are being generated uniquely by us rather than understanding that our uniqueness is in constant interaction with all that surrounds us to the most expansive degree that we can conceive of.

I have a strong sense that these very words I am writing are pulled through me by the desires of a small or large number of people to have certain questions answered via my interpretation of how to structure the answers given. We are relating to each other's "frequency signature".

It’s like finding someone who “speaks your language”.

I have heard many authors and artists express that they love the feeling of aliveness that comes from expressing that which they are inspired to express. There is a sense or knowing that one is answering a calling. So when someone says they feel a calling to do this or that, I believe that is literally true.

As each party thinks about a specific idea, the attention to that thought form is energized, and therefore, it expands its ability to broadcast and receive. That amplified signal travels further ahead, and then that many more people whose frequency matches will pick up on it for the first time, and most likely experience it as “their idea”.

If there is sufficient desire for the expression of such a thought form, one or several people with the capacity to bring that thought form into physical creation will experience a spark that compels them into action. Therefore, they are the ones who will be credited for the idea.

I think this is very similar to an electrical storm. As the static energy builds up, it looks for a spot that offers the greatest capacity to accept the charged-up energy. When this happens, we experience it as lightning.

To put it another way, when there is enough of a connection between a thought form and an entity capable of carrying it to the next stage of development, a pulse of energy (inspiration) will strike one or more people, similar to a single or multiple strikes of lightning. Having received such an impulse, the beneficiaries are now so fully energized by that "idea" that they feel compelled to make an effort to bring it into physical form. This, I believe, is how the same invention can show up in different places at almost the same time. How many times have you heard someone say, “It hit me like a bolt of lightning”?

I believe that a need or unanswered question creates a void in the universe and that the universe always seeks to fill such a void by drawing out a creative response.

The greater the consensus upon that need, the bigger the void, and, hence, the stronger the pull for a solution that will eventually manifest the birth of new thought forms. Of those thought forms, the ones that receive the most consensus are the ones that will be sparked into action and fulfillment.

Magnetic Energy Relative To Thought

The following is really just another way of explaining the concept of how thought forms work.

Most people know that a magnet has a positive and a negative pole, and that if one breaks a magnet in half, one doesn't get a positive end and a negative end. One gets two smaller magnets, each with a positive and a negative pole.

No matter how many times the magnet is split in half or what size the pieces are, the end result is smaller and smaller magnets, each with a positive and negative pole, and each becoming progressively less powerful.

The same phenomenon holds true for joining them back together. Even when the weakest of magnetic forces gather together, they grow stronger. The larger the magnet, the more powerful it becomes whilst retaining just one positive and one negative pole.

I believe that our collective thought process works in a similar fashion. Once a thought form is created, it will emit a unique frequency which, by the terms of our universe, will broadcast and receive its frequency signature, the strength of which is based on its mass. Whenever we give attention to a particular thought form, we add to its mass.

Positive Influence

Without regard as to how all of this happens, there is a medium by which we receive and project thoughts. Its existence has been unequivocally demonstrated in multiple human-to-human and human-to-animal experiments.

Is communicating through our universal frequency field meant to be our primary means of communication? Where does the outer edge of that possibility lie, and once understood, how much power can we exert by conscious collaboration of thought?

Just as a mirror reflects a true image, the universe delivers back to us the exact frequency signature we broadcast. Just as a waiter delivers the food that we ordered, the universe will also, without judgment, continue to deliver our request. If we want something different, we have only to change our frequency.

If we feel that despite changing our frequency, we keep getting the same food, we must trust and be grateful for the truth of the feedback. Let us also agree that it is not really fair to get mad at the waiter, for when we place a different order, the waiter will deliver our request.

When we take the time to focus on, or tune in to, beautiful, positive, peaceful, or loving thoughts, we emanate those frequencies, and therefore, attract more of the same.

By aligning ourselves with positive frequencies, we can experience two forms of benefits—personal and global—while also sensing that we've just made a positive contribution to those present within our field of influence.

When we have the good fortune of benefiting from others' positive efforts, we are lifted up and gain a new perspective. Life becomes a little easier and the path forward looks more promising. This further illustrates the multiple benefits that are created by any kind of positive contemplation.

We all tend to reject and avoid being manipulated, even when the one seeking to manipulate us has noble intent. Rather than applying thought or intention to try to create a specific action or response from someone else, some practitioners have concluded that the most effective means of contributing towards a positive outcome is by focusing on elevating oneself.

They believe that in doing so, the subject will radiate a higher frequency which will help to lift all those around them, just as a rising tide lifts all boats. From that point forward, onc is encouraged to trust that the person one is seeking to influence will, from that more elevated position, be able to see the best way forward and will make the best decision for all concerned. This point is illustrated very well in the book *The Secret of Shambala* by James Redfield.

We are definitely affected by each other's frequencies. Merging waves can either cancel each other out or combine to become larger and more potent. We have all had the experience of someone walking into a room and just lighting it up, and conversely, sometimes the room lights up when someone leaves.

Sometimes, we lose ourselves to the task. As an example, I was once so intensely involved in blazing a new trail through the brush that I forgot to make sure whether I was going in the right direction. I know that I have done the same thing many times, just in less obvious ways.

When we observe some of us veering off course, it is important to remember that, like all of us, they are doing their best. Since we are all functioning through subconscious patterns of behavior passed down through generations, we all have the opportunity to feel compassion. We need to do our best to respond to the circumstances by remembering that they too are good people who have simply gotten a little too over-focused on a different issue.

In such a situation, one can help to create conscious action by going into a peaceful state. By doing so, you will be broadcasting peaceful frequencies to those around you, in a kind of beautiful melody.

If, however, we are the beneficiary of such an uplifting frequency, we also might experience it as a cool breeze on a hot day. Upon doing so, we would feel compelled to stop for a moment, expose our face to it, inhale deeply a few times, and enjoy a moment of peace. In that moment, we regain perspective and our actions are either affirmed in the direction we are going, or we notice a more attractive path.

When such an event happens, be sure to take a few seconds to be grateful and know that while you are doing so, you are also benefiting all within the field of your influence.

Just by thinking about anything that you are grateful for, you will immediately feel the benefit and, by the laws of nature, that frequency will spread to others. When they respond in a similar fashion, you will have helped to create what is called a "positive energy spiral".

Spending time in appreciation is a form of meditation, and I've found that meditating for even a few minutes in the morning tends to change my state of mind for the whole day. When I do so, I am more likely to stay tuned in to what I have to be grateful for, and, in that state of mind, everything around me seems to work better.

As a more condensed statement: When we notice someone's struggle, we feel compassion and want to help. By taking a moment to simply appreciate them for making the effort to find the best way forward, we are radiating a harmonic, supportive frequency that will make a difference. If we take just a few more moments for an on-the-spot, mini-meditation, then even though we would benefit from it, the frequencies and uplifting energies we radiate will have the effect of that gentle breeze upon those within our field of influence.

I know that I have been the beneficiary of such wonderful moments created by others. Likewise, they have sometimes contributed towards major turning points in my life.

A small course correction can have a huge impact on where one eventually arrives.

Our Global Mind

While working on expanding our perspective, we can think about this “universal frequency field” I’ve referred to within the framework of the global mind. Many individual cells make up our brain/body, which in turn sustains our mind. Likewise, I believe that as individuals, we are like the cells of a global brain/body, and as such, we are all-sustaining and contributing to the global mind.

Our brain/mind emits measurable wavelengths that change depending upon our state of being. As we move from producing beta to alpha to delta and theta waves, we move towards deeper states of meditation, peaceful feelings, and even euphoric states of oneness.

If you accept that we do have the ability to be connected to each other as well as to animals, where does the outer edge of that connectivity lie?

If we are a collection of small magnets that make up a much bigger field, can we still consider ourselves to be independent? Or are we a group of interdependent beings that contribute to and operate through the collective field?

The evidence leads me to conclude that we are all truly interconnected. I believe we are all participants in a global mind, and therefore, we must also have some personal knowledge of who we are as a collective body.

Just as a little thought can make its way from the back of our mind to the forefront of our consciousness, I believe the same happens within the global mind/community. A small idea can turn into a global movement.

When you pick up on a positive thought that you would like more of the world to experience, focus on it for a while, enjoy it, and visualize more people doing the same. It feels good to do so, and that feeling is a confirmation that you are in alignment with your higher self. The more ways to feel good you can find, the better for you. Moreover, your efforts make it that much easier for the rest of us to have the same experience.

I am reminded of a health resort I was once a co-owner of. It had a round exercise pool with a round island in the middle. We would have participants run in the same direction through the waist-deep water, and very quickly, the current seemed to be carrying everyone along. What currents would you like to give energy to? Positive thoughts generate positive currents.

Our thought forms are like seeds in the wind. Some fall on fertile ground and receive vital water under favorable conditions while others turn to dust. Water and nurture only those thought forms which you desire to grow.

Growing Ourselves

Since we function on auto-mode throughout most of the day by going through the necessary motions, just like a ship that moves towards a pre-defined destination, how do we get the captain to come back into the wheelhouse?

Whatever we appreciate tends to grow. So, to start with, spend time acknowledging and appreciating those super-awake moments whenever they occur. Another way to tap in to that frequency is to contemplate past moments of joy or love. If you spend 30 seconds to a couple of minutes doing so, you will definitely start to experience that bright-eyed, fresh, awakening feeling.

At times, we are the ones helping to move the current. We know we are in the flow and can feel our contribution. At other times, we might feel the current moving us, such as having a sense that we are being gently pushed forward in a new direction. If we feel exhausted and hopeless, it means we are fighting the current. We feel truly at peace when we flow with the current.

If we "get" that we are here to be of service to each other, it becomes easier to find our direction. Once we learn to trust and act on the inspirations we receive, we will experience "flowing with the current". When we remain "in service", we will experience a sense of fulfillment of purpose.

Responding to and aligning with the frequency that creates the most harmony is our way of finding our current part in the symphony of our life.

If you've ever heard someone tuning an instrument, you understand the discomfort of being out of tune. Without making the effort to change, we are unlikely to play in harmony. However, when we do come into tune with others, we experience the relief and joy of harmonious frequencies.

Finding our way into the greatest service is how we tune ourselves, and providing that service is like playing in56 in56 a symphony. Feel the joy of playing your individual part and allow yourself to feel the power and majesty of being a part of something greater than yourself.

Whenever I feel better for whatever reason, I take the time to feel and express my gratitude. In doing so, I am energizing and expanding that frequency. I feel more tuned-in, and I know that I've just made a positive contribution to the whole.

We All Have An Ego

Each one of us has the ability to be a positive influence on our personal and global world.

We seek to make our lives better and we like to be recognized for our achievements, partly out of pure ego, but partly out of a desire to show others a better way forward.

We all have an ego, and as long as we remind ourselves that our ego is only one aspect of our "self", it is reasonable to allow our ego to be encouraged in a positive direction.

We and our egos tend to focus on what makes us different from others, such as their weaknesses against our strengths. Doing so can serve a healthy purpose until we become so overly focused on what separates us that we lose touch with the commonality that sustains us.

When we come from a place of appreciating others' successes and see ourselves as building upon their inspirations, we fall in alignment, and as such, we experience and radiate harmonic frequencies.

There are obviously great benefits to discovering a way to build better widgets or finding ways to become more efficient to complete this or that task. That desire to go for and get "the gold sticker" is a great part for our ego to play.

When we come from a place of destructive criticism, anger, and exclusion, we end up disrupting the integrity of our frequencies and radiate those disruptive frequencies to others.

By having an inclusive approach whereby we gratefully acknowledge and appreciate each other's strengths as assets to the whole, it becomes much easier to sustain health and well-being, both personally and globally.

Are We Helpless Victims?

To make my point, I need to touch upon an earlier subject. Until we were around seven years old, we, like a dry sponge, absorbed all that we were exposed to, and whatever we absorbed solidified to become our underlying rationale for how to respond to life.

There are those who use this kind of information as an excuse to continue to play the part of a helpless victim, powerless to change their life and destined to suffer life's reactions to how they were programmed. However, such behavior is a choice.

People who choose this approach serve as evidence of the misery that comes from following it. We must be grateful that we are "the witness to" rather than "the participant in" such a process.

When asked, "If you could change your past, what would you change?" people may initially say, “sure, I would like this and I would have done that.” However, upon further contemplation, most will conclude that they would not change anything.

They usually go on to say that each event, no matter how unpleasant, provided them with the insight and character they now possess. They will further state that these hard-won assets are what have allowed them to contribute to the world around them more effectively.

Instead of dwelling on past mistakes, we must understand that, at every event in our life, we have made the best decisions we were capable of given our prior programming of how to respond to such events.

We must repeatedly tell ourselves this: We did the best that we could do. We did the best that we could do. We did the best that we could do. We did the best we could with the information we had to work with; or we would have made better decisions.

Those whom we might blame or carry anger towards were in the same position. They too were doing the best they could with how they had been programmed.

It is not a matter of condoning our inappropriate actions or those of others. It is a matter of gaining perspective.

A child may be fascinated with throwing sand into the wind while being oblivious to what those downwind may be experiencing. At some point, that sand will blow into the child's own eyes, providing a valuable lesson about air currents, sand, eyes, and pain.

From a distance, we understand the process. We understand that learning involves both joy and pain, for ourselves and for others. We revel in a child's joy, we empathize with their pain, and we feel close to that little being as our memories take us to our own childhood moments.

This combination of the distance required to gain perspective and the closeness of our own experience creates compassion, love, and appreciation.

We always have the opportunity to replace our judgments about our individual and collective struggles with forgiveness, compassion, and love.

The sum total of our previous life experiences ends at this very moment, which is also the beginning of the rest of our life.

Every one of our experiences forms the building blocks of who we are now. As we respond to life, those building blocks are the sole source of stored information that we have to draw from.

We learn from our mistakes, and my history has demonstrated to me that each “mistake” was to prepare me for a time when the information and humility gained from it was worth the pain of the mistake. While suffering/recovering within the midst of a mistake, I've learned to trust that the day will come when it will become crystal clear to me that experiencing "the mistake" was necessary to prevent a much greater calamity later down the line.

Sometimes the only reason we find ourselves following the path of least resistance is due to having bumped into obstacles on either side. However, there is another way to avoid many of the scrapes and bruises that come with that approach that I have come to sincerely appreciate. That method involves taking the time to contemplate which way to go, by moving in the direction that feels the best.

We each have a unique combination of foundational skills that has prepared us to be of service in a way that only we can do. The more aligned our actions are with the fullness of what we have to offer, the greater the sense of personal fulfillment.

I recently heard a story from a man whose friend called him to say that he was about to commit suicide. The man's loving and compassionate response demonstrates the power of service.

The man responded to his friend by saying, "Can you think of anyone who needs help in any way?" His friend thought for a moment and then responded, "There is an older woman in my apartment building with all sorts of garbage and leaves in front of her door." The man then said, "While I wait on the line, please go clean it up for her. I will be here for you when you get done, so please go do it now." After 15 minutes or so, the friend came back on the line and said, "I feel so much better. I started to feel better as soon as I began helping her." He went on to express his gratitude and stated that he could now see a clear path towards a more fulfilling life through being of service.

Rather than being helpless victims, we are the beneficiaries of the experiences, information, and finetuning needed to contribute to the universe we live in.

We have so much to offer each other and often, it is the little gestures that have the deepest impact.

When we act on those little impulses to do something nice, we tune in to a frequency of love and joy, and that's kind of a nice place to hang out.

Who Is It That Answers?

When you ask yourself, "Should I say this?" or "Should I do that?" do you get a response?

Most of us don't really characterize that internal dialogue as a relationship. However, I believe that it is of utmost importance to develop a very good, honest and compassionate on-going dialog with the part of you that answers these questions. Talk about "a long-term relationship"!

The degree to which we have true compassion and appreciation for ourselves is the degree to which we are able to have compassion and appreciation for others.

When you observe or experience yourself or others doing things that you do not like, celebrate the awareness and be grateful that you are, in that moment, far enough above the density to be the observer rather than the participant.

Only when we realize how much of who we are is based upon previously accepted programming, will we have the freedom to choose new programs.

To swing on the monkey bars, one must have a firm grip on the next bar before one lets go of the previous one. Similarly, we have no chance of letting go of familiar habit patterns (programming) until we have formed new ones to grab hold of. Otherwise, the fear of falling will lock us in our previous position. In most cases, such a fall would be only a couple of inches instead of the bottomless canyon that our mind builds it up to be.

The more that we accept ourselves and let the current move us along, the sooner we feel a part of, and a contributor towards, the force of that flow. In truth, we are always a part of the flow. Only our feelings of separation keep us from experiencing that flow.

One of the most effective ways of implementing change is to take the time and effort to seek out experienced self-help practitioners, enroll in self-help courses, or simply ask people to share the secret to their success. Each of those ideas has the possibility of returning rich, life-altering benefits.

Many of us have an underlying fear that if we change our programs, we will lose who we know ourselves to be. Firstly, we need to respect and acknowledge the power that such fear has to lock us in a fixed mindset.

Secondly, we must recognize that as long as our fears are hidden, they possess the greatest influence on us. Conversely, when we bring them into the light of day, what we perceive to be a mountain usually turns out to be only a little molehill.

Any learning process modifies our programming, and most of the time, we do change in some small way as a result. The soul/observer part of us judges what to keep and what to let go of. That relationship is the one most worthy of your attention as *you* will be with you even after you lose your current form.

Reprogramming

There are reasons to be disappointed and there are reasons to feel full of appreciation. Which state of being feels the best to you?

Have you been subconsciously programmed to believe that worrying or feeling bad is somehow more real than feeling good? What would you think of someone who spent their whole time on vacation feeling bad? Are we on vacation? Is this your life? Are you having a good time?

Some people have a wonderful time wherever they are. Doing so is simply a learned behavior. If you don't like the behavior pattern that you are wearing, try on another one.

Certainly, a chemical imbalance can stand in the way of a happy life. However, there are many more avenues through which one can seek and achieve help than what are commonly suggested. Even fairly extreme cases of autism have had dramatic improvements through nutritional interventions. Penicillin was being used for 12 years before it was commonly accepted. Where do you want to be on that scale? There could easily be just as effective solution for an issue you are aware of, that you don't know about.

We are in a constant state of evolving our thoughts. Collectively, we are gaining new information every single day. When you are ready to take responsibility, reach out for help and pay attention to and act on the guidance that you receive. Your world can change in ways that will amaze and delight you.

You can either hope for new information to just drop into your lap, or you can become your own personal advocate. By actively researching what has worked for others, you can find yourself getting closer to the cutting edge of discovery. Your expanding mind will inspire others to do the same and you will have the pleasure of directly passing along your research to those you care about.

Even when you pass along some of the most amazing discoveries, please don't be surprised or too disappointed if people don't act on what you have given them, because that seems to be the rule rather than the exception, even when faced with certain death.

Our minds are so securely locked into the realities that we have accepted as "the way that it is", that it is rare to find an unlocked door or window, even when you see them looking back at you through the glass.

Those are the times when it is critical to understand that we are all playing our special parts for many more reasons than we understand. Frustration and pain come from expecting other people to play their part as if you were writing the script of their lives. Instead, play the part you are cued to play, and as in watching any new play or movie, observe with fascination how others are cued to play theirs. This is the path to peace and love.

Our internal recording media contain our whole life experience. Everything that we take in simply adds to who we are and gives us a bigger base of information to draw on for making choices.

Sometimes, memories of certain past experiences have the emotional volume turned up so high that they permeate our lives. Post-Traumatic Stress Disorder (PTSD) is one example of just how disruptive that raging volume of emotion can be.

We all tend to have examples of past events that keep taking up too much space in our lives, maybe even more than we know.

There are very effective and simple techniques for dramatically reducing that volume or intensity of emotion, while retaining the memory of those experiences for future reference.

Every movie in the library of your personal history has an emotional volume control. When the volume is up too high on one movie, it is hard to access the experiences stored in other movies, or even truly experience the new ones currently in production.

Of the many successful methods for adjusting that volume, two of my favorites are EFT (Emotional Freedom Technique) and Edu-K (Educational Kinesiology). Both are simple and truly unique, and both offer far-reaching and long-lasting benefits.

I am very grateful to have had the benefit of so many positive contributions to my life, starting with my family lineage. Apart from family, two important influences that stand out at this moment are Napoleon Hill, who was mentored by none other than Andrew Carnegie, and Abraham-Hicks Publications, although there are many other very significant contributors.

If you ever find yourself regretting not knowing about this or that much earlier in your life, you will be falling into a common and insidious little trap. Access humility, know that for whatever reason the timing was not right until it was and move into gratitude that you are there now.

Please remember that focusing your attention on disharmonious thoughts is akin to watering weeds when the new seeds of your life are what deserve your love and nurturing.

Being Grateful

Being grateful for the gifts of our lives will carry us through the toughest of times and will create more to be grateful for.

There are always many reasons to be grateful. However, it is easy to ignore them when you are distraught. To avoid this, start with being grateful for your little toe (if you are fortunate enough to have one), and then for the rest of your toes, your foot, your ankle, etc. I have been far enough down to start with my little toe a few times in my life, so I know this works. By finding anything at all to be grateful for, other reasons will begin to flood in like the dawn of a new day.

I believe that "being grateful" is the most effective way of improving your life and the lives of those around you.

Because of how intimately we are all connected, the way in which each of us spends our time makes a difference to those “close” to us in both senses of the word. Again, the degree to which you appreciate and love who you are is the degree to which you will appreciate and love the rest of us.

We Are All Toddlers

We all seem to harbor guilt for any number of reasons and think that by doing so we are somehow making restitution.

We must always remember that at any given moment, we are doing our best. We can criticize ourselves and say, “I could have done better,” and that may be true in hindsight, but it was not true in that moment, or you would have made a different decision.

At some level, we are all still learning by testing what works and what doesn’t, similar to how a toddler does its best to navigate its body and learn about what is acceptable and what is not. Is it right to send a toddler on a long guilt trip for breaking a dish or spilling this or that when they did not have the basic input to make a better decision?

In one way or another, we are all still toddlers relative to what we will know in the future. And we have our past to prove it. So, I ask, is it fair to go on a guilt trip when you did not have the necessary input to make a better decision?

This perspective is important for each of us to recognize and appreciate, for by doing so, we can reconnect with our innocence and spend more time in a state of forgiveness, appreciation and love for ourselves.

Whenever we find we are being hard on ourselves or feeling guilty, we must take the time to recognize the truth of the situation. Doing so will help us understand that we made the best decision that we could with the information we had to work with in that moment. Our harsh feelings will melt away into forgiveness and love for the toddler that we were and are even now. Such efforts lift us, and those elevated frequencies emanate towards those close to us, which helps them to grasp the same concepts without us saying a word.

Lastly, once we have accepted we were/are doing our best in any given moment, we will start to automatically recognize the same is true for everyone we interact with. Sometimes, it is challenging to truly believe that, but how many times in our lives might someone else believe the same about us. Be grateful for the new awareness and simply drop the judgments about others who are less fortunate in that moment.

Are We The Instrument Or The Symphony?

Does distance make a difference with a TTE? Who initiates the connection, and who is the one responding? Does it matter?

Individually, we are one instrument within the grand symphony of the global experience. All members of the symphony are doing their best to perform their parts. In effect, each is performing a solo that, from a distance, is experienced as one glorious sound.

We all operate independently with our personal specialties. We each have specific parts to play that are also, somehow, integrated into the interdependent make-up of the whole.

So, what is it that you want to support? What are you watering with your attention now? Remember, whenever we are focused on the weeds of our life or of this world, we are helping those thought forms to grow. Whatever we are fighting against (focused on) becomes a bigger and stronger thought form.

Our perception of how the world works is greatly influenced by how we were programmed from the very beginning. Our security lies in our identity, and our identity is all about how we fit in, and how we fit in is completely tied to what we know the world to be.

Our basic subconscious core resists any ideas that might undermine the foundational concepts that we have built our life upon, and probably for a good reason. Without such a governor, life might be just a bit too helter-skelter.

Our subconscious controls most of our daily life, so there are only short parts of each day when our more curious, conscious mind has a chance to introduce change to the subconscious. As a way of creating cultural stability, the subconscious mind seems to change only through repetition. It takes focused effort for our conscious self to create true change in the subconscious programming.

It turns out that having an open mind can be a little challenging because of the very nature of our being. We seek the security of normal and are "open" only to new things that fit within that realm.

Anything that happens outside of "normal" will be labeled by our culture as such and will be defined in such a way that prevents it from challenging the present "norm". That dynamic is a societal survival technique designed to create cohesiveness. Normal is comfortable and, understandably, we like comfort.

This is the reason that, collectively, we have been so determined to treat the "telephone thing" as a novelty, or to explain and accept a "miraculous recovery" by saying, "Sometimes these things just happen."

We "self-medicate" by setting such events on the religious shelf, which somehow takes them out of the realm of needing to have any other answers. Once placed on that shelf, it is much harder to gain permission to dissect and discuss the issue, as doing so could be perceived as an affront to God's grace.

We are currently on the threshold of accepting a truth which, to date, has been considered too disruptive for our Western culture to fully embrace.

One hundred years from now, upon reviewing our current culture from a distance, I believe students will ask, "What kept them from believing what they directly experienced?"

I think they will conclude that we were so enmeshed in the belief system of our collective subconscious mind that we simply did not have permission to go there.

At some point, we will have collectively experienced enough "coincidences" that our collective logic will have no choice but to conclude that these events are more than "coincidences". I believe we are in the midst of that event now.

When we experience a consciousness-raising event, the foundation upon which our beliefs stand is altered. Initially, we find ourselves in unfamiliar territory, so we feel a little insecure. Our senses heighten, and we regain a sense of familiarity. Then our senses relax, and we are now fully adjusted and comfortable with the change. By the time this sequence is completed, we are one mini-magnet closer to making that same shift as a culture.

If the completion of that sequence involves a major change in the way we interpret our world, it's called a "paradigm shift".

Many of our conclusions about life are based upon assumptions that eventually turn out to be incorrect. Even so, because we are so anxious to strengthen the foundations that support the shaky security of our beliefs, we continue to treat assumptions as absolute truths.

Until recently, scientists observing herds of elk believed that the decision to head for water was made by the alpha male. Through time-lapse photography, it has now been determined that when one of the elks is ready to go to the water, it faces in that direction and keeps grazing. As soon as the majority of the elk are turned in the direction of the water, the whole herd starts to move in that direction.

To me, that is a small and simple example of how a paradigm shift happens. In such an event, the balance of those who had been resisting a change seems to act as if the new way is the same way that it has always been.

We have empirical evidence that prayer can reduce the mortality rate and increase the recovery rate from heart attacks. We have absolute evidence that we can pick up on each other's thoughts, and that animals can do so as well.

What might we achieve if, as a nation or as a global community, we fully acknowledge what we are already experiencing? Do all animals see the pictures in our minds? Is this one of their methods of communication with each other? How would the integration of such information affect our everyday lives? Do we have the ability to consistently create our own prescriptions through the power of suggestion? Can we discover how to completely heal ourselves by focusing our minds? How might our hospitals change? Will we learn to hone our communication skills to the point that future generations rarely use a telephonic device?

When will scientists announce that they have discovered the medium that allows the transference of mental images from one being to another? Where will that lead us?

It all starts with trusting what we know. Once we give ourselves permission to believe in the truth of our experience, we will feel confident and will be at ease with the subject matter.

Many of us have had truly uncommon and profound experiences, or at least we think they are uncommon. Such experiences are also very liberating.

Unrecognized mental boundaries fade like the morning fog to reveal new and exhilarating possibilities for personal expansion.

When the timing is right, sometimes I will very gently open the door to this subject matter with business clients by bringing up TTEs.

I have noticed that when I do this, some of my clients share profound experiences of their own that have no commonly held scientific explanations. These revelations, in combination with others gathered over time, have led me to conclude that what is "common" is our collective hesitation to talk about such events, whereas if we did, we would realize just how common they are.

When there is an air of acceptance and validation, people long to acknowledge and share that which has altered the very foundation of how they "know" life to be. It is as if they have a pocket full of gems that they desperately want to reveal but will only do so upon demonstration of trust.

Too often, deeper contemplation of a profound experience causes our minds to become overwhelmed with destabilizing questions. As a means of re-stabilizing, our mind does its best to put that experience in an unmarked box and place the box in a cubby in the farthest corner of our mind.

Until we are willing to be honest with others about the truth of what we experience, we will keep the current “normal” in place.

Over time, more holes will form on the movie screen onto which we project the status quo. The more involved we are in the movie, the longer it takes to notice the holes. When something distracts us from the content of the movie, our concentration is broken. Upon our efforts to refocus, the holes start to become obvious. We generally do our best to get used to the holes again so we can continue where we left off. Eventually, our curiosity gets the better of us. Our attention shifts to the holes, and we suddenly realize that there is much more to reality than the projected images we had accepted as real.

Once we clearly acknowledge the holes, we can be on our way to discovering the new "normal" screen. Eventually, that new screen will develop holes, and the same process repeats itself, which is our evolutionary process.

As constant as the movement of the heavens, we are growing—individually, culturally and globally. I believe a future historian will find this time period to be very similar to the beginning of the European Renaissance, and I am truly excited to witness and participate in this major paradigm shift to a new understanding of the power of thought.

Wrapping It Up

I felt inspired to put these thought forms in writing and I believe that you were a part of the collective request to do so. You and anyone else who reads these pages for any reason had questions from your conscious or subconscious mind that have been addressed in some manner through what has been shared here, or you would not have been inspired to read these words.

It may be that some things have been validated for you. It may be that you have become more aware of some questions that need answers, or it may be that what has been shared here will be of some benefit later down the road.

I can sense where we are going as a culture and I felt the pull to validate some thoughts and stimulate some others. I am grateful to have had this little part to play and am excited about what comes next.

It is possible that these words might have been for the benefit of just one person—me. I got a lot out the experience.

How many are benefited is not important. What is important is to respond. I felt compelled to act, or, as I like to describe it, I was cued to play my part. I love the transitional moment between receiving the cue and acting. Within those few seconds, I experience being moved by something greater than myself and such experiences validate my purpose for being here.

The process of writing this book was insightful. Most of the time I felt that I was collaborating with a mentor to express our collective perceptions. I sensed a strong, loving, compassionate, and intelligent energy flow that was somehow sourced through the contribution of others. It was as if you, the readers, were asking the questions and my life experiences put me in a position to act as facilitator, which was very fulfilling.

I believe what I experience. And those experiences have led me to trust in “the way of things”.

I trust in the love that is life, and I do my best to grow and share.

I believe that a charismatic member of the popular media will sponsor an event that demonstrates, in a tangible way, our collective ability to elevate others.

The results of that demonstration will bring us trust and have confidence that such efforts are worthy of duplication. Consequently, many others will be inspired to create similar events that, in turn, will create just that much more tangible evidence, leading us along an upward spiral of consciousness.

Several weeks after I wrote that statement (this has been a work in progress), Oprah launched an international consciousness-raising event. I am not aware that anyone was trying to track any measurable changes, such as crime rates or increases in generosity, although I am confident that many of us were benefited.

I sincerely appreciated Oprah's, or anyone else's, willingness to make such a contribution for the benefit of all. Any time someone does something new, they are very vulnerable to criticism. I doubt that most people really appreciate just how much courage it takes to be on the leading edge. I loved that I was tapping into that frequency pattern, and I know there is much more to come along the same lines in many ways.

This is not new information. I have simply presented it in a way that a certain portion of our collective mind requested.

Each piece of the mystic puzzle reveals the hints and clues needed to complete our shift to this new paradigm for the power of thought.

I believe that the day is not far off when we will fully embrace and understand what we now refer to as "medical miracles" as tangible, repeatable events. When that happens, such knowledge will become fully integrated into our hospitals as "standard operating procedure".

By acknowledging our true ability to communicate, we will become much more adept and confident with our skills.

Having come this far, if you are now feeling inspired to play your part in this little shift in perception, all I can say is to continue to feel it, trust it, believe it, and act on it.

Do you trust and love who you are? Do you accept that toddler aspect of yourself and offer unconditional love to yourself at any age, including now?

By the terms of nature, you are seeing this world through the filter of your subconscious mind. You are, and have been, doing your best, just as the rest of us. Be compassionate!

Trust your heart. Bring fear into the light. Forgive yourself and others for mistakes made, for only then will you truly be able to accept the beautiful and magnificent evolutionary being that you are.

I thank you for your courage, for your conscious effort to "take the wheel" of your life, and for actively seeking that which feels better. May you do so until the end of your days!

What gift does this day hold for me and what part in someone else's gift will I play?

—Sam R. Buck III

A Few More Thoughts To Pass Along

Worry:

When we worry, we project a thought pattern to someone we obviously care about. In doing so, we communicate to them the following thoughts: I do not trust you. It is likely that you are going to make a mistake, get hurt, hurt someone else, or in some other way, create failure.

At some level, they are tuned in to your frequency and will pick up your broadcast. From the recipient's side, one of the most important people in their lives is demonstrating, in a subtle yet very powerful way, a complete lack of confidence in their judgment. What does this message do for their self-confidence and self-esteem?

Here is another possibility for how to use the same amount of your energy:

Project that your loved one will have a wonderful time, make great decisions, and gain valuable insights. From the recipient's side, one of the most important people in their lives is now demonstrating, in a subtle yet very powerful way, complete confidence in their judgment. Imagine the impact this kind of messaging would have on their self-confidence and self-esteem?

Which is the better message to send? How might such a change affect your relationship?

We always radiate what we feel. Are you feeling anxious and nervous, or relaxed and confident? If you were sending your loved one out to perform on-stage, which emanation do you think would help them to perform their best?

If you really think about it, the odds are fully with the positive projection. In the very rare event that something unfortunate does happen, you can choose to trust that the lessons learned will help them to avoid a bigger pitfall later in life.

It does take focused effort to change your habit patterns. That is all that they really are, replaceable learned behaviors. Such interpersonal work elevates you and allows you to contribute to the rising tide that elevates us all. The reward is similar to completing volunteer work. You know that, in your own way, you have made a difference and that feels great.

If you now understand, at a conscious level, that you are always projecting your internal "mental emotional state of being", you will also understand how important it is to be responsible for your energy. Take it lightly. This is not a burden, but an opportunity to grow and contribute.

Like it or not, in some aspects, we are still at the toddler stage. It takes practice to learn new skills. Have patience, love yourself, and keep moving towards the energy patterns that feel right.

Children:

Our children are literally the foundation of our future. Yet we treat so many of them more like cattle, herding them along from one pen to the next.

Now is our opportunity to stimulate innovation and create positive change. With proper attention, each child can tap in to their tremendous potential and create positive impacts on society.

I visualize a culture that recognizes and nurtures many learning styles, understands that children's brains develop at different rates, and realizes that at each stage of development the child has enhanced abilities to absorb specific subject matter.

I see children learning multiple languages, tactile applied mathematics, and artistic expression through exposure to what is interesting to them, rather than what is on the curriculum. We want to stimulate their brains, stir their desires, and help them grasp the tangible benefits of learning so that they are inspired to want to know more.

Compare a young mind that becomes overwhelmed with meaningless data points to one that is engaged in a subject that creates a thirst to know more. Think about the impact of maintaining that level of thirst throughout their school experience.

- What would those graduates accomplish?
- What would happen if we insisted upon nothing less?
- How confident would you be in our collective future under those conditions?

The development of our human potential presents our best opportunity to create a better world.

Everyday Votes:

Make your everyday votes count, feel the power, and exercise your will to create your vision of the world.

I want to inform and empower you to realize that you have the ability to lead even the biggest of corporations towards your way of seeing things.

Every dollar you spend is a vote that they absolutely pay attention to. Think of how many times you vote every week. When you purchase a product or service, you state to the purveyor, "Yes, I approve of what you are providing and please create more of the same."

Think about the impact you can have every time you purchase earth-friendly products. For instance, buying organic produce has multiple and far-reaching effects. Not only do you get higher nutrient values, you also consume fewer toxins. The handlers of the produce are safer, the growers are safer, and the water runoff into our creeks, streams, rivers, lakes, aquifers, and oceans is safer. Additionally, individual and collective healthcare costs are reduced, the positive bacteria that break down minerals for assimilation by plants and bugs can flourish, all of which supports the birds, fish, all other wildlife in our environment. How powerful is that! Now multiply those efforts across your state, country, and the world.

We must also realize the impact of the difference we make by using bio-friendly cleaning products over toxic products. What we put down our drains via laundry, sinks, showers, toilets, or runoff from our streets, gardens, and lawns will end up in our septic drain fields, sewer systems, street drains, and drainage ditches, and ultimately end up in our water supply and oceans.

Many of the most troublesome and long-lasting toxins pass right through our municipal sewage treatment plants and septic drain fields, as these systems are primarily designed to keep us safe from nasty pathogens like bacteria and viruses.

Think of the far-reaching impact you can have by using your dollars to vote for cleaning, gardening, and lawn care products that are environmentally friendly.

Our rivers, lakes, and oceans are becoming so polluted that dead zones are rapidly expanding. There is such tremendous momentum in the direction of using heavily-advertised toxic products that it can seem hopeless. However, with your help, change will happen. Pay attention and act. Every vote counts and each one is timely.

Corporations are committed to making money. If they notice that sales are dropping off in one area and picking up in another, they will follow that trend and will do their best to stay ahead of the competition. What we see on the supermarket shelves is what we have collectively asked for. When we change, they try to catch up by test-marketing, which is a way of asking us if they are moving in the right direction. Sometimes they try to fool us, but eventually we find out and they lose their credibility as well as our vote in favor of a better product and a more honest company.

Suppliers are little more than dust in the wind without us. We control them by voting with our dollars and they "follow the money". It used to be that they made it and we bought it. Now, thanks to the actions of those with conscious vision, we have choices.

I happily bought Kellogg's Organic Raisin Bran, Mini-Wheats, and Rice Krispies just to communicate my pleasure to them and to the store that was carrying their product. The fact that they produced them is evidence that our votes absolutely make a difference. The amount of acreage that was dedicated for that purpose alone prevented tons of toxic products from entering into our ecosystem, and I applaud them for doing so.

There are stronger and weaker definitions for what organic means, and the stronger, the better for us all. I encourage active support of all efforts that move us in the right direction. If we keep buying the best we can find, the market will follow.

There are also stronger and weaker definitions for biodegradable or environmentally-friendly products. Take the time to read a few labels or look up some product reviews. With only a little effort, you will get a sense of who is providing the most valuable product or service.

I've recently learned that most fragrances in soaps (including organic, high-quality essential oils) along with all surfactants (all soaps and wetting agents), are very toxic to our marine environment. So please use unscented products and natural coconut oil or olive oil-based surfactants (all I know of for now) as they break down fairly fast. Most, if not all, of the other synthetic surfactants take a very long time to break down, and therefore, by a large factor, they kill many more small marine animals that are critical to the food chain.

I learned this from a four-hour class my wife and I took from a highly respected chemistry professor named Russell Barsh of KWIAHT (Center for the Historical Ecology of the Salish Sea) wherein he demonstrated the negative impacts of surfactants and fragrances even at highly diluted levels of ten parts per million.

There may be some fragrances that are not toxic, and there may be some other alternatives that are safe. As of this moment, even what seemed to be the safest, most bio-friendly soaps were still toxic even at highly diluted levels.

I know that this is disturbing information for most of us who have been doing our best to use the most environmentally-friendly products.

The awareness will create more desire for better answers and eventually, someone will come up with a great answer, maybe even you.

Another way to contribute is by buying concentrated products. The more concentrated a cleaning product is, the more loads per packaging, which means fewer trucks per load of laundry. Fewer truckloads lower the negative side effects of shipping via energy use, pollution, etc.

Here is a big THANK YOU to those individuals and their companies that broke, and continue to break, the difficult ground.

Hopefully, you now understand that every time you vote with your dollar, you radiate a frequency that contains the whole awareness that led to your vote. Please understand and feel the far-reaching implications of making such conscious decisions. You are so much more powerful than you think you are.

We, individually and collectively, have the ability and the choice to create the world that we want to live in.

Determine your course and express your will through conscious action and deed. Appreciate and honor the passion and dedication of those who came before us.

Each step in the right direction feels good and we know that others will benefit from our efforts as well.

We must have raindrops to create a stream and many streams to create significant and unstoppable flow. Every effort you make is a contribution towards what you desire to be.

Would you be impressed, and a little in awe, if someone told you they had just completed a journey that has taken them 19, 33, 82, or more years to complete? You know you would, so be impressed with yourself for the length and content of your journey.

Think of the experience you've gained and how much wiser you are for it. I truly congratulate you!

You are, at this very moment, at the pinnacle of your life experience. You are both at the end of the life journey that led you to this moment, and at the beginning of the life-enriching journey ahead of you. What a great place to be!

***

I sincerely thank you for who you are in this wonderful universe and for the contribution that you're making towards the betterment of all that is.

Your heart drew you to read this book, or it would not have happened. I appreciate you for being the brave pathfinder that you are for your soul's journey and for the sake of those who feel you. It may come to pass that our hearts will be able to directly smile at each other. However, even at a distance it is wonderful to connect.

—Sam R. Buck III

To learn more about the people and techniques referred to in this book, please explore the following websites:

Abraham-Hicks Publications	www.abraham-hicks.com
Bruce Lipton	www.brucelipton.com
EFT (Emotional Freedom Technique)	www.emofree.com
James Redfield	www.celestinevision.com
Larry Dossey	www.dosseydossey.com
Rupert Sheldrake	www.sheldrake.org
Institute of Noetic Sciences	www.noetic.org
Louise Hay	www.louisehay.com
Joe Dispenza	www.drjoedispenza.com

www.ingramcontent.com/pod-product-compliance
Lightning Source LLC
LaVergne TN
LVHW012102160826
845678LV00014B/2905

* 9 7 9 8 3 6 2 9 5 2 3 8 9 *